AND TH

Remembering the World of Anne Frank

by

JAMES STILL

10

Dramatic Publishing

Woodstock, Illinois • England • Australia • New Zealand

IMPORTANT BILLING AND CREDIT REQUIREMENTS

All producers of the play must give credit to the author of the play in all programs distributed in connection with performances of the play and in all instances in which the title of the play appears for purposes of advertising, publicizing or otherwise exploiting the play and/or a production. The name of the author must also appear on a separate line, on which no other name appears, immediately following the title, and must appear in size of type not less than fifty percent the size of the title type. Biographical information on the author, if included in the playbook, may be used in all programs. In all programs these notices must appear:

"Produced by special arrangement with DRAMATIC PUBLISHING COMPANY of Woodstock, Illinois"

"*And Then They Came for Me: Remembering the World of Anne Frank* was originally commissioned and produced by the George Street Playhouse, David Saint, Artistic Director, and Young Audiences of New Jersey, Kristin Golden, Executive Director."

"Original George Street Playhouse/Young Audiences of New Jersey video was directed by Susan Kerner and created by Susan Kerner in collaboration with James Still."

* * * *

WHAT PEOPLE ARE SAYING about *And Then They Came for Me*...

"This was one of the most moving experiences I've had as a director (25 years). I followed each performance with a Q & A with actors/audience/and a holocaust survivor. It was incredible."
Jane Talley, Bishop Gorman High School,
Las Vegas, Nev.

"What a wonderful venue (sic) for combining theatre and video arts. The story of Eva and Ed is just striking enough to be shocking and human enough to be moving." *Janine G. West,*
Boulder High School,
Boulder, Colo.

"The play *And Then They Came for Me* changed the lives of my cast. Even after months of research and preparation, the actors came to me after opening night with stories of the impact it had on their lives. We will never forget it."   *Michael Ruth Penwell, Johnson Bible College, Knoxville, Tenn.*

"A challenging & rewarding play. Afterwards, audience members thanked us for our courage to do this show—they also stated that every high school should perform it."   *Chris Solmon, Dyersburg High School, Dyersburg, Tenn.*

"Our audience, cast and crew will never be the same. This powerful drama taught us more about the Holocaust than books. When you see and hear two survivors telling you their story it becomes very personal to everyone. This is educational theatre at its finest."   *Carol Svoboda, Lincoln Southeast High School, Lincoln, Neb.*

"This is extraordinary, thought-provoking look at a time in our history that should continue to give us great pause— many of the issues at the root of these horrors are still very much issues we are dealing with today. Our audiences were deeply moved by this multimedia theatrical event."   *Rosalind Allen, Oaks Christian School, Westlake Village, Calif.*

"The show was extremely successful. It was thought provoking and emotional. It caused my students to think about the past & ponder the future and be concerned about what we are doing in the present. It was one of our best productions."   *Jo Ann H. Taylor, Avery County High School, Newland, N.C.*

"*And Then They Came for Me* is the most powerful theatre-for-youth production that we have ever mounted. It is a beautifully crafted play that provides insight into a horrible time in our history. Extremely moving!"   *Catherine Rodgers, Meredith College, Raleigh, N.C.*

* * * *

"After the war people said it would never happen again, and people didn't want to talk about it—it was something that happened, let's forget about it, now we live a different life. What's happening now in Bosnia and what's happening in many other places—but Bosnia I say because it's Europe—we're still doing the same thing and again the world just looks on."

— Eva Schloss

"Take heed...lest you forget the things which your eyes have seen, and...teach them to your children and to your children's children."

— Deuteronomy 4:9

"Forgiveness is a personal matter. You have the right to forgive what has been done to you personally. You do not have the right to forgive what has been done to others."

— Simon Wiesenthal

"History has a way of becoming history."

— Ed Silverberg

This is a play about questions. Some of the questions seem unspeakable. Admittedly, many of the questions are unanswerable. Even so, that doesn't diminish the importance of asking the questions.

Although there are many philosophies and passionate points of view within the field of Holocaust Education—please approach this as a play—not as a "Holocaust play" but as a play about people who lived during the Holocaust. It is a subtle yet important distinction. This is not a "history play"—it is a play about families and their histories.

I am a writer who vividly remembers reading Anne Frank's diary the first time at the age of 12. Something stirred inside me—still stirred inside me years later as I worked on this project. I hope that as the years continue to faithfully mark all of the anniversaries connected to World War II—that audiences will remember Anne and Ed and Eva and their experiences as young people during the Holocaust. The only way that we will remember the Holocaust is if we hear from the people who were actually there. Then, I'm convinced, we'll never be able to forget.

Like most plays, *And Then They Came for Me* has had its share of loyal champions who have helped make the play possible when it mostly seemed impossible. The list is long and the fingerprints are many. There are a handful of people, though, that I must mention by name.

Thank you to Kris Golden, Stephen Mosel, and Susan Kerner for hiring me to write this play in the first place.

Thank you to Grayson Covil and Megan Boothby at the Anne Frank Center USA for suggesting that we contact Eva Schloss.

Thank you to Diane Claussen for never giving up on all of the thorny issues surrounding a very complicated process.

Thank you to Gary Glickman for believing in the importance of this project and lending a generous heart and a smart eye through its many, many drafts.

Thank you to Janet Allen and the Indiana Repertory Theatre for believing in the play before there was much of a script to believe in, and for the gift of that first production.

Thank you to Rives Collins and Graham Whitehead—to your casts and productions—for helping me see the play again through your fresh, generous eyes.

Thank you to Tom Werder for wading through stacks of papers, playing catch-up and embracing this project during a time of transition.

Thank you to Gayle Sergel for being the editor that all writers dream of…you told me you were in this for the long haul. Thank you for meaning it.

Thank you to Susan Kerner for passionately walking beside me as I worked on this play, and for directing the first several productions around the country. I will always cherish your devotion to this project.

And thank you to Eva Schloss and Ed Silverberg for talking to a kid from a small town in Kansas who was born years after the war ended, for trusting me with your precious stories, and for teaching me more than you'll ever know.

— James Still

After the war, when my mother and I returned to Amsterdam, I found it very hard to accept that my father and brother were never to come back. From that moment I have had a special dream. It was that our family, which had so cruelly been destroyed, would be reunited again, even if it were only in a film, or on the stage.

So, when Susan Kerner approached me out of the blue, to ask whether I would be interested to cooperate in a play about several Holocaust families, I knew that my dream was coming true.

Meanwhile, I had become increasingly involved in Holocaust Education. I have spent much time talking to young people especially, mainly in schools. I fear greatly that the lessons of the past may be forgotten, if only because we all tend to push aside what is unpleasant. Therefore it seems to me very important that the surviving witnesses should continue to testify.

I welcome the success of *And Then They Came for Me* for both these reasons. It allows me to share my family with audiences all over the U.S.A., and hopefully soon in other countries too. Also, the memory of the Holocaust is recreated vividly and convincingly in the play. I have watched very many performances and each time have been very moved by the deeply felt interpretation of the young actors and their portrayal of the humiliation, degradation and pain our families had to endure. The strong impact on the audience, which is visible after each performance, comes as no surprise.

I am very fortunate to have been privileged to work with a playwright as gifted and as sensitive as James Still and with as inspired [a] director as Susan Kerner. Many thanks to them also for having given me the opportunity to meet so many wonderful people involved in various ways with the creation and performances of the play.

— Eva Schloss, 1999

And Then They Came for Me has given me the opportunity, after fifty years of relative silence, to reflect on and to speak about my experience as a young boy during Hitler's Holocaust years.

In 1942, at the age of 16, I befriended Anne Frank for a few short weeks before she and her family went into hiding. For me she has come to represent the many school friends and childhood playmates who perished at the hands of the Nazis.

It is my hope that the publication of this moving play will enable an ever-growing audience the world over to carry on the memory of Anne Frank. It is, after all, the next generation that must keep alive the knowledge of this dark episode in human history, so that it may never be repeated...

— Edmond Silverberg, 1999

In addition to many documentary films, fiction and non-fiction books about the Holocaust, and time spent in Amsterdam, which included a visit to the Anne Frank House, this play has primarily been adapted (with permission) from the following sources:

Eva Schloss: from taped interviews with Mrs. Schloss in Edgware, Middlesex (London) on November 26 and 27, 1995. Interviewer – James Still.

Ed Silverberg: from a taped interview with Mr. Silverberg in Hackensack, New Jersey on August 3, 1995. Interviewers – James Still, Susan Kerner, Kristin Golden.

The videotaping of Ed Silverberg and Eva Schloss occurred on May 21, 1996, in New Brunswick, New Jersey.

And Then They Came for Me premiered at Indiana Repertory Theatre in Indianapolis, Indiana (Janet Allen, Artistic Director), on October 2, 1996. Direction was by Susan Kerner. Scenic design by Robert Koharchik; costume design by Jeanette deJong; lighting design by Betsy Cooprider-Bernstein; music by Scott Killian; video editing and design by Stephen Datkowitz; archival photographs and footage researched by Susan Kerner; video sound effects by Bill Milbrodt. The stage manager was Sabian Trout. The cast was:

Young Ed, Pappy . . . . CHUCK GOAD
Young Eva, Ed's Mother . . . . MARITA CLARK
Anne, Mutti . . . . CRISTEN PAIGE
Hitler Youth, Heinz, Ed's Father. . . . . TOM MEUNIER

In a revised script, *And Then They Came for Me* opened in South Brunswick, New Jersey, presented by George Street Playhouse Touring Theatre (Susan Kerner, Artistic Director) and Young Audiences of New Jersey (Kristin Golden, Executive Director) on November 2, 1996. Direction was by Susan Kerner, scenic design by Robert Koharchik, costume design by Barbara Forbes, original music composed by Scott Killian, editor/electronic visual design by Stephen Datkowitz, archival photographs and footage researched by Susan Kerner, lighting design by Brenda Veltry, sound design by Bill Milbrodt. The stage manager was Amy Williamson. The cast was:

Young Ed, Pappy . . . . DEREK JAMISON
Young Eva, Ed's Mother . . . . KAREN ZIPPLER
Anne, Mutti. . . . . MICHELLE SPIRES
Hitler Youth, Heinz, Ed's Father . . . . JOHN SOCAS

George Street Playhouse in association with Young Audiences of New Jersey presented *And Then They Came for Me* on the Main Stage at George Street Playhouse opening on April 25, 1997. Direction was by Susan Kerner. Original music composed by Scott Killian; set design by Robert Koharchik; costume design by Barbara Forbes; lighting design by Brenda Veltre; editor/electronic visual design by Stephen Datkowitz; archival photographs and footage researched by Susan Kerner; video sound design by Bill Milbrodt; production sound design by Michael Shawn Deiger. The stage manager was Thomas L. Clewell. Production manager was Edson Womble. The cast was:

Young Ed, Pappy . . . . RON SCOTT
Young Eva, Ed's Mother . . . . KAREN ZIPPLER
Anne, Mutti. . . . . MICHELLE SPIRES
Hitler Youth, Heinz, Ed's Father . . . . JOHN SOCAS

* * * * * *

Recommended reading: *Eva's Story* by Eva Schloss. "A patently honest account of the struggle of a courageous and resourceful young woman to survive in a nightmare world." *(Jewish Chronicle)* This book is available in North America from Dramatic Publishing (800-448-7469). The book is available in the UK from Eva Schloss, 91 William Court, 6 Hall Road, London NW8 9PB.

This play is dedicated to
Eva Schloss, Ed Silverberg, and their families.

And Then They Came for Me is obviously based on Eva and Ed's experiences as young people during the war...but it was listening to their voices, watching their faces as they told me their stories from fifty years earlier—that continues to inspire me, haunt me and move me. I know that they do not think of themselves as heroes—but to me, that is what they were. And by choosing now to share their stories with young people and their families—Eva Schloss and Ed Silverberg are heroes again.

AND THEN THEY CAME FOR ME:
Remembering the World of Anne Frank

A Full-length Play
For 5 Men and 4 Women
(minimum 2 Men, 2 Women with doubling)

CHARACTERS

YOUNG ED	HEINZ
ED'S MOTHER	MUTTI
ED'S FATHER	PAPPY
HITLER YOUTH	ANNE
YOUNG EVA	

Doubling suggestions

6-actor version:

ED
EVA
PAPPY / HITLER YOUTH
MUTTI
ANNE / ED'S MOTHER
HEINZ / ED'S FATHER

4-actor version:

YOUNG ED / PAPPY
YOUNG EVA / ED'S MOTHER
ANNE / MUTTI
HITLER YOUTH / HEINZ / ED'S FATHER

14

AND THEN THEY CAME FOR ME:
Remembering the World of Anne Frank

(The setting is simple. A make-shift curtain has been pulled across the length of the stage. It is a a tattered curtain, crudely hung. It suggests that something hides behind it—a stage, a window, secrets. There is no other adornment, no other clues.

A YOUNG BOY—12 years old—hurries on stage, out of breath, excited. He sees the audience and addresses them directly, as if he were talking to a friend. As he talks, he is putting on a uniform—one piece at a time. He dresses in front of us, casually transforming himself as he talks.)

YOUNG BOY

X. up right

This is the greatest country in the world! No more unemployment, no more inflation, no more workers on strike, no more violence in the streets. My father says big government is to blame for our problems. And the Jews. And the immigrants, the Blacks, the homosexuals, the mentally and physically handicapped... RATS are the lowest form of ani-

VIDEO IMAGE:
Red background

mals, and the JEWS are the lowest form of mankind. If we can get rid of the Jews the world will be a better place. That is what the Führer says. *Heil, Hitler!*

SOUND: Mass "Heil Hitler!"
VIDEO IMAGE: Swastika
VIDEO IMAGE: 1930s Nazi rally in stadium
VIDEO IMAGE: Hitler in car

I've been a member of the Hitler Youth since I was seven. *Heil, Hitler!*

SOUND: Mass "Heil Hitler!"
VIDEO IMAGE: Children saluting Hitler

(German nationalist music begins low and builds; YOUNG GERMAN VOICES overwhelm the stage.)

VIDEO IMAGE: Adults saluting Hitler

We say *"Heil, Hitler!"* if we meet a friend on the way to school. We say *"Heil, Hitler!"* at the beginning and end of every class. The Postman says *"Heil, Hitler!"* The woman who sells us groceries says *"Heil, Hitler!"* If our parents don't say *"Heil, Hitler!"* we are supposed to report them and they will be arrested.

VIDEO IMAGE: Children saluting Hitler

VIDEO IMAGE: Hitler saluting
VIDEO IMAGE: Child saluting Hitler

(German BOYS and GIRLS —hundreds and thousands of voices join in.)

SOUND: Children's voices reciting:

HITLER YOUTH & CHILDREN'S VOICES
"I promise at all times to do my duty for the Führer, so help me God." November 9, 1938. Germany needs you! *Heil, Hitler!*

(Sounds of thousands of youth cheering. The YOUNG BOY has completed his transformation into a YOUNG HITLER YOUTH. As he runs out, he rips down the curtain which reveals a stage filled with posters, placards—slogans all written in German. The cheering crowds and German music fades away. We begin to hear the sound of boots. Boots marching in unison. Order. Hundreds and thousands of boots. Then the sound changes to boots trampling. Chaos. Breaking glass. And dogs barking. German Shepherds. Vicious barking. We hear voices in the distance shouting commands in German. Then we hear

SOUND: Cheering crowd: "Heil Hitler."

SOUND: Boots marching, tanks firing, tanks passing.

SOUND: Breaking glass
SOUND: Dogs barking

SOUND: German commands
More marching
More tanks

the sound of knocking on a door. Then banging on several doors. Banging so loud it sounds as though the building will collapse. The German voices sound as though they will burst on stage. Now the voices are suddenly children, teenagers.)

SOUND: Knocking on door

SOUND: Banging on doors
SOUND: More German voices

GERMAN VOICES

Sau Juden! Verfluchte Mistbienen! Schnell! Schnell! Raus ihr Mistbiene. Verfluchte sau Juden!

SOUND: German young

(Total silence. On projected screens, the video image of ED SILVERBERG appears. He is in his late 60s. He addresses us directly.)

ED

My name is Helmuth Silberberg. I was born in 1926 in Germany and later moved to Holland to escape the Nazis. My nickname is "Hello" which is what Anne Frank called me in her diary. *When I was a teenager I escaped again and hid from the Nazis in a townhouse in Belgium.* That's how I survived the Holocaust.

ED ON VIDEO

Onstage, *YOUNG ED speaks simultaneously*

(The image on the screen changes to EVA SCHLOSS. She is in her 60s and addresses us directly.)

EVA

My name is Eva Geiringer Schloss. I was born in Austria in 1929. *When I was a teenager I was in hiding for 22 months in Holland. I was arrested by the Nazis and spent nine months in the Auschwitz-Birkenau concentration camp.* I am a Holocaust survivor.

EVA ON VIDEO

**Onstage, *YOUNG EVA
speaks simultaneously***

(The CAST OF ACTORS gather around the images of ED and EVA on video and asks questions.)

FIRST ACTOR

What was it like to live through that?

SECOND ACTOR

How did you survive?

THIRD ACTOR

What made the Nazis so cruel?

FOURTH ACTOR

That could never happen again…could it?

(The ACTORS are drawn to the stage by ED's and EVA's images on the video screens telling their stories.)

ED

My grandfather who lived in Germany in 1933 happened to be on a business trip in Amsterdam, and the day Hitler was elected he called my grandmother on the telephone and told her to sell everything, he's not coming back to set foot in Germany. He understood something that…some people did and some didn't.

ED ON VIDEO

EVA

When the Germans entered …the Nazis entered Austria in March 1938, suddenly things became…quite different. Friends which we have had for years didn't want to know us anymore.

I couldn't understand why suddenly I'm different from my friends. And um… It was something which I really couldn't grasp.

EVA ON VIDEO

ED

There were people such as my father who thought that this would blow over. The idea being that the German people—the German people would never allow this to go

ED ON VIDEO

on, they're civilized, this cannot happen here, this is as far as it's going to go. And he belonged to, unfortunately, to a group of Jewish people who—who were wrong.

VIDEO TITLE: "1938"
CHASER TITLE: "Germany"
SOUND ON VIDEO:
Camera snapping
VIDEO IMAGE: Ed as a
young schoolboy at desk

(YOUNG ED, ED'S FATHER, and ED'S MOTHER pose for a series of family photographs. There is a bright flash of light.)

SOUND ON VIDEO:
Camera snapping

ED

…a car pulled up with a group of thugs, they were civilians from different areas with sledge hammers and various other devices—

ED ON VIDEO

(The sound of glass breaking. Chaos. ED'S FATHER flees. ED and his MOTHER huddle together.)

SOUND ON VIDEO: Chaos,
car pulling up, screeching
brakes, shouting…
SOUND: Glass breaking
V.O.: GERMAN VOICES

*NOTE: Additional sound on sound CD to play simultaneously.

YOUNG ED

Are they gone, Mother?

(ED'S MOTHER walks quietly to the front door, to see if the intruders are gone.)

YOUNG ED

Mother?

(ED'S MOTHER gestures for him to be quiet.)

ED

My mother was at the door, was hit with a sledgehammer over the shoulder.

(ED'S MOTHER is hit by an unseen German. She crumples to the ground. YOUNG ED goes to her.)

ED ON VIDEO

SOUND: Door breaking, German voices, crashes, boots walking, *"Ferdunt Juden!"* "Filthy Jew!"

YOUNG ED

Mother? Did they hurt you?

ED'S MOTHER
(touching her shoulder, her face)

They hit me…

YOUNG ED

I know… I—I didn't know what to do. They had sledge-hammers and crowbars,* they were drunk—

ED'S MOTHER *(overlap)*

*They hit me…

YOUNG ED

They were yelling, smashing furniture, *they even cut the carpets—

ED'S MOTHER *(frantic)*
*Your father! *Where is your father?

YOUNG ED *(overlap)*
*They didn't get him—

ED'S MOTHER
Did they take your father?

(ED'S FATHER runs on and ED'S FAMILY embraces.)

ED'S FATHER
I'm here.

ED
We had…a flat roof in back
of where we were living, my
father was able to get out
there.

We have often wondered
about the reactions of our
neighbors who witnessed
some of this. And uh…I
don't really know, I am certain that uh, there were people in Germany who were
abhorred by this—Germans.
But not much was done to
help the Jews.

ED ON VIDEO

ED'S FATHER
It's best if you go to your grandparents' for a while.

YOUNG ED

They won't come back, Father. We haven't done anything wrong. It's a mistake… You said yourself—

(ED'S FATHER hands his son a suitcase. This is very difficult.)

ED'S FATHER

It's too dangerous, son. We don't know what's going to happen.

YOUNG ED

What do you mean?

ED'S MOTHER

You'll be safe in Amsterdam with your grandparents. *(She kisses YOUNG ED, doesn't want to let go.)*

ED'S FATHER

We'll join you as soon as we can.

(YOUNG ED nods, turns to go, stops and looks back at his parents, terrified.)

ED'S FATHER

If you get scared, remember our secret whistle, yes?

(ED'S FATHER softly whistles a line from Beethoven's Ninth Symphony. With his mother's encouragement, YOUNG ED half-heartedly joins in. The three of them whistle together. For a moment it feels safe again. The whistling fades out. There is nothing and everything to say. YOUNG ED's parents wave goodbye and disappear. YOUNG ED looks around, begins to whistle again—alone.)

Something catches his eye and he stops whistling. He stops in his tracks and watches, as Ed On Video narrates.)

ED

I knew how to get by street-car to the railroad station. And on the way I saw the Essen synagogue in flames, burning. And people from the fire department standing nearby and doing nothing.
I was 12 years old.

ED ON VIDEO

SOUND: Fire

(YOUNG ED gets on a train.)

ED

I didn't have a passport at that age but I had an I.D. card with my name and…

ED ON VIDEO

(Sound of a train whistle.)

SOUND ON VIDEO: Train whistle, train station

YOUNG ED

At the Dutch border, two guards wearing SS uniforms ask me to step out of the train…

VIDEO IMAGE: SS Border guards

SS BORDER GUARD #1
(drawing out the name for emphasis)
Silberberg???

V.O. ON VIDEO:
SS BORDER GUARD

SS BORDER GUARD #2   **V.O. ON VIDEO:**
  He's a child—   **SS BORDER GUARD**

SS BORDER GUARD #1   **V.O. ON VIDEO:**
  He's Jewish!   **SS BORDER GUARD**

  (YOUNG ED watches fear-   **VIDEO IMAGES: SS Guards**
  fully, as if looking up from
  one BORDER GUARD to
  the other, waiting for them
  to decide his fate. They be-   **V.O. ON VIDEO:**
  gin to argue in German.   **SS BORDER GUARDS**
  This continues under:)

      ED *(V.O.)*
Something happened—I   **V.O. ON VIDEO: ED**
never knew what—

(SS GUARDS V.O. out.)

       ED
—at the other end of the   **ED ON VIDEO**
station platform—and they
walked away.

       YOUNG ED
  And I got back on the train. By the time I reached my
grandparents' home in Amsterdam they had no idea what had
happened in Germany.

       ED
I always felt at first they   **ED ON VIDEO**
really didn't believe me…
why I was there.

PROJECTED TITLE:
"Kristallnacht"

DISSOLVE TO SEPARATE
IMAGE: "Night of the
Broken Glass"

YOUNG ED

But the next day it is on the radio and in all of the newspapers: the German Kristallnacht—Night of the Broken Glass—had destroyed Jewish businesses and burned synagogues. Thirty thousand German Jewish men and boys were arrested and sent to concentration camps. I have no idea when I'll see my parents again. Or even IF I'll see my parents again. I am lucky to be with my grandparents in Amsterdam. *(Beat.)* For the moment, I am in a safe place.

VIDEO TITLE: "1938"
CHASER TITLE: "Austria"

EVA *(V.O.)*
My brother Heinz looked
rather Jewish—

V.O. ON VIDEO: EVA

EVA
And different from me with
blonde and blue-eyed…and
um, so everybody knew he
was Jewish. And um…

EVA ON VIDEO

EVA *(V.O.)*
His friends from his school,
from his class attacked him
one day. And he came home
all bleeding, his nose and his
eye was cut.

V.O. ON VIDEO: EVA
VIDEO IMAGE: Eva and
Heinz on bicycles

(HEINZ rushes on with a bloodied face.)

YOUNG EVA
Heinz! What happened?

HEINZ
They attacked me!

YOUNG EVA
Who?

HEINZ
I was at school, I was just standing there, *I wasn't even—

YOUNG EVA *(overlap)*
*School? But who would do—

HEINZ
They were friends, just kids at school. They called me a filthy Jew and started hitting me.

YOUNG EVA
Why didn't you tell the teacher?

HEINZ *(looking at EVA)*
Eva! He was there. My teacher watched the whole thing.

YOUNG EVA
Mutti!? *(Not wanting to believe.)* What did he do? Surely he stopped the…

HEINZ
He watched. And then he walked away.

YOUNG EVA

Mutti!!!

EVA

This was the situation in Austria at the time.

EVA ON VIDEO
SOUND: TRAIN

(MUTTI [Eva's mother] and PAPPY [Eva's father] enter with suitcases. The family stands together.)

MUTTI

We leave Austria and immigrate to Belgium.

YOUNG EVA

And then we move again.

HEINZ

And again.

PAPPY

We're trying to stay one step ahead of the Nazis.

YOUNG EVA

By 1940 we settle in Amsterdam, Holland, where my father thinks we will be safe.

VIDEO IMAGE: Amsterdam —houses along the canals

VIDEO TITLE: "1940"
CHASER TITLE: "Amsterdam"

(Eva's family. YOUNG EVA and HEINZ stand against a wall as PAPPY marks their height on the wall with a pencil. MUTTI watches hap-

VIDEO IMAGE: School photo of Eva as young girl

pily. The mood is lighter,
safer.)

PAPPY

Every month we will measure you and see how much you have grown. *(Touches EVA's face.)* You'll be safe here. We'll all be safe here.

MUTTI

You're growing so fast, Evi! We'll have to have that dress lengthened...

EVA

There was a dressmaker in   **EVA ON VIDEO**
our block where we lived
and we got there and she
said, "Can you just wait in
the hall."

YOUNG EVA

So I sit down and I hear a voice behind the curtain—a girl who sounds very determined...

(From behind a lit curtain we see the silhouette of a young girl.)

ANNE'S VOICE *(authoritative, no pauses)*

This dress would look much better with shoulder pads. Do you think the hem is all right this way? I think the hemline should be just a little higher. And shoulder pads. Definitely shoulder pads.

(The curtain is pulled away and ANNE FRANK models a new dress. She twirls around, showing it off for YOUNG EVA.)

EVA
It was Anne Frank.

EVA ON VIDEO

ANNE
Do you like it?

**VIDEO IMAGE: Snapshot of
Anne Frank as a young girl**

YOUNG EVA *(answering ANNE)*
Oh yes!

*(ANNE twirls around again and again and again. YOUNG
EVA watches ANNE as she continues to twirl/laugh as:)*

EVA
I didn't know, of course,
that later on I was going to be
asked questions about her,
because she became really—
a very famous person
through writing her diary.
  She was a very pretty girl,
very lively, talked a lot, gig-
gled a lot.

EVA ON VIDEO

**VIDEO IMAGES: Anne
Frank snapshot**

ANNE
(giggling, whispering, telling YOUNG EVA about the boys)
Eva! Is he looking at me?

YOUNG EVA
Who?

ANNE
That boy. Don't look! I don't want him to see us looking!

YOUNG EVA

Who is he?

ANNE

Just one of my many admirers. Do you like boys, Eva?

YOUNG EVA *(shrugs)*

My brother Heinz is a boy. He's perfectly nice.

ANNE

You have a brother? You're so lucky… I only have a sister. Margot—she's three years older than us— she says she doesn't really like boys—but I think she's just a big pretender. *(Seeing the boy again.)* He's looking again! And he has a friend. Maybe his friend is in love with you.

VIDEO IMAGE: Snapshot. CLOSE on Anne.

CAMERA PANS to include Margot Frank in photo. CLOSE on Margot. Fade out.

YOUNG EVA

I don't know…

ANNE *(refusing to take no for answer)*

You should talk to him.

YOUNG EVA *(awkward)*

I'm still so new, Anne, I can't speak Dutch yet— I'm…I feel…strange. Like I don't belong.

ANNE *(kind)*
Eva—you must come to my flat and meet my father. He can speak German to you.

(ANNE and YOUNG EVA go to Anne's apartment.)

EVA *(V.O.)*
Otto Frank—when I met him first—was a very tall, distinguished-looking gentle-man. He right away made me feel very much at home.

V.O. ON VIDEO: EVA
VIDEO IMAGE: Snapshot of Otto Frank

EVA
And he spoke to me in German which was wonderful for me because I had just been in Amsterdam perhaps for six weeks and I didn't speak the language, of course. I didn't suspect that later on he was to become my stepfather.

EVA ON VIDEO

VIDEO TITLE: "1940"
CHASER TITLE: "Invasion"
SOUND ON VIDEO:
Bombing, air raids, guns… invasion
V.O. ON VIDEO: ED

ED *(V.O.)*
The Nazis came in with their armies—

ED
—on May 10, 1940—

ED ON VIDEO

ED *(V.O.)*
—and occupied the Nether-
lands rather quickly.

V.O. ON VIDEO: ED
SOUND: Planes, whistle
bombs, explosions

EVA *(V.O.)*
After five days the Ger-
mans had won the war, they
bombarded Rotterdam and
the Dutch capitulated.
  So, and then we realized we
were really trapped.
  They started to take the
measures against the Jewish
population.
  So life became very, very
difficult.

V.O. ON VIDEO: EVA

VIDEO IMAGE: Nazi
armies marching, in
motorcades, in trucks

VIDEO IMAGE: Civilians
walking on sidewalks

YOUNG EVA
  Jews are not allowed to go outside after eight o'clock at
night.

HEINZ
Or before six o'clock in the morning.

ANNE
Posters and signs are everywhere.

VIDEO IMAGE: A sign that
reads: *"Die gelben Bänke*
sind für Juden"

YOUNG ED
Notices appear in the newspaper:

YOUNG EVA
Jews are not allowed to go
shopping in certain shops—

**VIDEO IMAGE: More
footage of civilians walking
streets**

ANNE
Only Jewish shops—

HEINZ
And only between the hours
of three and five p.m.

YOUNG EVA
Now Jews are forbidden to
attend theaters or the movies.

VIDEO IMAGE: Newspaper

ANNE
We're not even allowed to have a radio—

YOUNG ED
Which is terrible because the radio is the only place we get
information about the war.

ANNE
And music! I miss listening to music on the radio.

HEINZ
I had a little sailing boat on the Amstel river. But I had to
turn it over to the Nazis. Jews are not allowed to have boats.

YOUNG ED
Jews are forbidden to take part in any athletic activity in
public.

ANNE
You can do this and you can't do that…

YOUNG EVA

Jews are forbidden to visit Christians in their homes.

HEINZ

Christians are not allowed to teach us.

YOUNG ED

We have to leave our schools—

ANNE

We have to leave our friends—

HEINZ

We have to go to Jewish schools—

VIDEO IMAGE: Snapshot of Eva and friend on bicycles

YOUNG EVA

With Jewish teachers—

YOUNG ED

Jews are not allowed on public transportation.

ANNE

Now we can't ride the buses—

HEINZ

We can't ride the trains—

YOUNG EVA

We can only ride our bicycles.

YOUNG ED

Then we had to hand in our bicycles.

VIDEO IMAGE: Eva/friend/ bike fade out of photo

ED

By the time it became a very serious issue—a freedom-threatening issue—it was too late. There was nowhere, no place to go.

ED ON VIDEO

VIDEO IMAGE: **Yellow star with "Jude" written in middle**

EVA *(V.O.)*

Beginning on April 29, 1942, all Jews in Holland were required to wear the yellow star.

V.O. ON VIDEO: EVA

(Wearing a coat, YOUNG EVA stands impatiently in front of her mother who stitches a yellow star onto the coat. HEINZ stands nearby.)

YOUNG EVA

But why do we have to wear it?

MUTTI

It shows you are Jewish. You can be proud of it, there's nothing wrong with being a Jew.

(MUTTI hands YOUNG EVA the coat and she reluctantly puts it on. HEINZ hands MUTTI his coat and she begins sewing on his yellow star.)

EVA

It had to be sewn on, on the left-hand side of our garment, on exactly a particular spot.

EVA ON VIDEO

MUTTI

Every outside piece of clothing has to show the yellow star.

(YOUNG EVA pulls the coat off and throws it to the floor. MUTTI looks up, goes to her. This is serious business.)

MUTTI

Evi, listen very carefully. You must always wear the yellow star now. If you don't—the Germans could arrest you.

(MUTTI picks up the coat and holds it out to YOUNG EVA. She takes it. MUTTI exits. HEINZ goes to YOUNG EVA and talks gently to her:)

HEINZ

I was sitting outside with a friend talking—it was a hot day so my friend took off his jacket and he didn't have a yellow star on his shirt. An informer Nazi saw us and arrested my friend for not wearing the yellow star. He's never been heard from again. He was 16 years old.

(YOUNG EVA puts the coat on and the two of them exit together.)

ED

The Green Police would cordon off a block of apartment buildings in Amsterdam and go from apartment to apartment ringing doorbells, people would open, they would march in and look for young people.

ED ON VIDEO

(Loud knocking on a door.
Continue "live" knocking
under YOUNG ED.)

SOUND ON VIDEO:
Knocking

YOUNG ED

I was in my grandparents' bedroom when they knocked. The door to the wardrobe was open and I stood behind it. The police came in, looked around, looked in the wardrobe, but they didn't look behind the open door. They didn't see me. They left. By sheer dumb luck they just didn't see me.

VIDEO IMAGE: Anne's
plaid diary

ANNE *(with her diary)*
I received this diary from my parents for my 13th birthday. The cover is red plaid—it's the most beautiful diary ever. Hundreds of these blank pages. I can't imagine what I'll write in it. *(She thinks and then looks in her diary.)* Something unexpected happened yesterday morning. As I was passing the bicycle racks, I heard my name being called.

VIDEO IMAGE: Camera
pans written page of
Anne's diary

YOUNG ED

Anne?

VIDEO IMAGE: Snapshot
of Ed as a young man

ANNE

I turned around and there was this nice boy—

YOUNG ED

Anne?

(Thirteen-year-old ANNE turns around and looks at YOUNG ED. She holds her books close, unsure of what he wants. She smiles, open. YOUNG ED moves toward ANNE, somewhat shyly.)

YOUNG ED
My name is Helmuth Silberberg.

ANNE
I know. Your friends call you "Hello." *(Smiling, joking.)* Hello…"Hello."

YOUNG ED
Hello…Anne. *(Beat.)* I was hoping—I mean if it's all right with you, can I walk you to school?

ANNE
Oh yes! *(Suddenly playing it cool.)* I mean, as long as you're headed that way…

(Relieved, YOUNG ED joins her and they walk together. ANNE talks to the audience.)

ANNE
Hello is 16 and I think he likes me.

ED
I continued to see her on different occasions—some by coincidence and some on purpose.

ED ON VIDEO

ANNE *(to audience)*
I turned the corner and there he was—waiting for me

again. He pretended that it was just a coincidence. But I think it was on purpose. He definitely likes me.

VIDEO IMAGE: Snapshot of Anne outdoors in chair holding a hat

ED *(V.O.)*
The thing I remember most about her—besides her ability to communicate—is some of her body language…

V.O. ON VIDEO: ED

ED
When she was sitting in a club chair at my grandparents' home she would put her arms under her chin and lean forward, which could be interpreted as being flirtatious.

ED ON VIDEO

(ANNE sits in a chair with her arms under her chin, leaning forward and talking to YOUNG ED.)

ANNE
I was born in Germany but we moved here when I was four. I have all kinds of hobbies. I like music. I like making up stories. I have a diary. I have a cat named Moorjte.

(Hello/YOUNG ED stares at ANNE happily. ANNE waits for a reply and doesn't get one.)

ANNE
So…tell me something about you.

YOUNG ED

I come from Germany too. My parents are in Belgium, but there's no way I can get there now. So I'm living with my grandparents. They're kind of old-fashioned, they think you're too young for me.

ANNE

I'm 13!

YOUNG ED

I'm 16.

ANNE

I'll be 16 in three years!

ED

I don't know whether you can be in love at age 16, really, but I was certainly attracted to her.

ED ON VIDEO

(YOUNG ED stands, ANNE stands.)

ANNE

When will I see you again?

YOUNG ED

I can see you every Wednesday evening, Saturday afternoons, Saturday evenings, and Sunday afternoons. And maybe even more.

ANNE *(to audience)*

He definitely loves me! *(She takes one more look back at YOUNG ED, then exits.)*

ED

I think I was probably in
love with her. She seemed to
think so too.

ED ON VIDEO

EVA

My brother Heinz—he was
three years older than me—

EVA ON VIDEO

EVA *(V.O.)*

And we had a wonderful
relationship.

EVA

He was a very, very talented
person.

V.O. ON VIDEO: EVA
VIDEO IMAGE: Snapshot of
Eva and Heinz with
friends
EVA ON VIDEO

EVA *(V.O.)*

He wrote poetry, he painted,
he was a wonderful musi-
cian. He played piano, he
played guitar…

V.O. ON VIDEO: EVA

VIDEO IMAGE: Heinz
playing the guitar

(YOUNG EVA and HEINZ, late at night. YOUNG EVA is
restless. HEINZ strums a guitar, picking out a simple tune.
YOUNG EVA sits up.)

HEINZ

Did I wake you?

YOUNG EVA *(shaking her head)*
It's all right. I can't sleep anyway.

(HEINZ continues to play the guitar under:)

HEINZ

Sometimes I think I must already be asleep, that all of this must be a nightmare, that if I can just wake up—everything will be the way it used to be. Remember the way it used to be? *(YOUNG EVA nods.)* If I still had my little sailboat, I'd get in it and float away. Far, far away to a place where... *(His voice trails away; he stops playing guitar.)* Far away.

YOUNG EVA

And I'd go with you.

HEINZ

Something terrible is going to happen, Evi—

YOUNG EVA

No—

HEINZ

I can feel it.

EVA

In June 1942—in the morn-
ing—there came a card with
a post—which was very or-
dinary postcard, and it says
that—

EVA ON VIDEO

*(YOUNG EVA, HEINZ, PAPPY and MUTTI gather to-
gether. PAPPY holds the postcard, reading:)*

PAPPY

Heinz Geiringer has three days to report—

MUTTI

Why are they doing this?

PAPPY

...with a backpack and a few belongings—

MUTTI

It will be slave labor!

PAPPY

...that he will be transported to a work camp in Germany.

MUTTI

He's just a boy.

(MUTTI begins to cry. YOUNG EVA looks at HEINZ. PAPPY looks at the postcard, looks at HEINZ.)

HEINZ

Don't worry, Mutti. *(Trying to comfort his mother.)* They won't harm me if I work hard.

(HEINZ looks at YOUNG EVA. He is very scared.)

EVA

The Nazis went after the young people because they didn't want Jews to survive—especially young people who would be the parents, who would have children later, so those were the people they wanted to kill first. So that there would be no new generation of Jews.

EVA ON VIDEO

HEINZ

I don't want to go.

MUTTI
Of course you're *not going.

PAPPY *(overlapping)*
*You're not going. *(PAPPY looks at MUTTI.)* It's getting too dangerous. It's time we disappeared.

YOUNG EVA
What does that mean?

PAPPY
I've made arrangements for us to go into hiding—

YOUNG EVA
Hiding?

PAPPY
We're going to live with other people—

HEINZ
What other people?

YOUNG EVA
For how long?

PAPPY
Just for a little while, until the war ends.

MUTTI
A month, two months—

PAPPY
You will be with Mutti, Heinz will go with me.

YOUNG EVA

What???

PAPPY

Evi, four people are too many—

YOUNG EVA *(alarmed, overwhelmed)*

Why can't we all stay together?

PAPPY

It's too dangerous for a family to hide all four of us.

(YOUNG EVA suddenly hugs her father and refuses to let go.)

YOUNG EVA.

Pappy! I don't want to go without you.

PAPPY

Evertje, be a grownup girl now. *(Whispering.)* You must look after Mutti for me. God bless you and keep you.

(HEINZ and YOUNG EVA embrace; PAPPY embraces MUTTI; intimate.)

PAPPY

If we are in two different places there is more chance that at least two of us will survive.

(Each of them holding a small bag, they part, splitting into two families—YOUNG EVA and her mother, HEINZ and his father—and walk away in opposite directions. YOUNG EVA and HEINZ look back at each other one last time.)

EVA

We didn't tell anyone about our plans of course because you never know who would betray you.

My family and the Frank family went probably into hiding the same time.

EVA ON VIDEO

YOUNG EVA *(alone)*

Hiding? What does that mean? Where will we hide? With who? For how long? Why can't we all stay together? And what about our home? Will someone else live there? Look out our windows? Sleep in my bed? When will we come back? What about my friends? What will happen to them?

ED

My entire friendship with Anne was limited to 1942.

ED ON VIDEO

(YOUNG ED goes to a door and rings the doorbell.)

SOUND: Doorbell

ED

One day I was due to come to her home on a Sunday afternoon, and rang the doorbell, and there was no answer. I can't tell you exactly what I thought. But you have to understand—that it was not unusual for people to just disappear.

ED CONTINUES ON VIDEO

YOUNG ED *(to older self)*
Maybe they got away. People can get away.

(YOUNG ED rings the   **SOUND: Doorbell**
doorbell again.)

ED
I recall that I was very   **ED ON VIDEO**
taken aback, that I was sad
about it, not seeing her.
I had seen her that morning
but that was the last time I
saw her.

YOUNG ED *(to himself)*
Maybe they got away.

*(YOUNG ED walks down the street by himself. Maybe he
whistles. He stops and looks back at Anne's house one last
time. He continues on. He doesn't look back. YOUNG EVA
and MUTTI appear—without the yellow stars on their
clothing.)*

EVA
My mother and me left in   **EVA ON VIDEO**
the morning and went right
across Amsterdam to go to
this new place, where we were
going to stay with a school-
teacher—Mrs. Klompe.

YOUNG EVA
Our contact from the resistance came to visit us and said we
must have a hiding place WITHIN our hiding place.

MUTTI

He decided we should make a false partition at one end of the bathroom and tile it with a little trapdoor.

YOUNG EVA

A hiding place WITHIN our hiding place.

MUTTI

They work very late one Sunday night until they finish it...

YOUNG EVA

They leave and we go to bed...

EVA

And in the night we heard suddenly lorries outside and shouting and knocking on the doors.

EVA ON VIDEO
SOUND: Lorries
SOUND: Knocking/shouting

(The sound of loud knocking on doors.)

YOUNG EVA

And my mother and me—we quickly jump into our new hiding place, we put the trapdoor on—

EVA

And my mother sat on the toilet and I sat on the floor next to her—*and waited.* And a few minutes later we heard the Germans with their heavy boots clomping up the stairs and my heart was beat-ing so loud that I was sure

EVA ON VIDEO

*MUTTI simultaneous: "And we wait."

SOUND: Boots on stairs

they would hear it through
the partition.

YOUNG EVA
We hear them opening the
bathroom door.   SOUND: **Opening door**

MUTTI
We hear them come in.
                                        SOUND: **Boots, near**

YOUNG EVA
We hear them looking.
                                        SOUND: **Boots walking
                                        around room**
MUTTI
We hear them searching.

YOUNG EVA
We hear them talking.
                                        SOUND: **German voices**

MUTTI
We hear one of them say,
"Nobody's here."

YOUNG EVA
They're walking away.
                                        SOUND: **Boots walking
                                        away**
MUTTI
Out of the room...
                                        SOUND: **Boots**

YOUNG EVA
Down the stairs...
                                        SOUND: **Boots down the
                                        steps**
MUTTI
Out of the house.

YOUNG EVA
The door slams.

**SOUND: door slams
downstairs**

MUTTI
They're gone.

EVA
And this is something when
I talk to you about it now I
feel it as if it's still happening.

EVA ON VIDEO

MUTTI
We're safe.

YOUNG EVA
But I can't sleep for the rest of the night. The sun comes up.
And it all begins again.

*(There is the sound of a tick-   **SOUND: Ticking clock**
ing clock.)*

YOUNG EVA
In hiding, the minutes turn into days turn into weeks turn
into months... I'd give anything to be able to walk in the
fresh air again, to feel the sunshine, to be free.

*(YOUNG EVA and MUTTI sit at a table in silence. The
ticking clock persists. MUTTI reads. YOUNG EVA tries to
read. YOUNG EVA fidgets. MUTTI looks up. They look at
each other. YOUNG EVA looks as though she may scream
or run from the room. MUTTI puts a finger to her lips as
if to say "Shhh!" YOUNG EVA looks at her watch. They
both go back to reading their books. The clock ticks
louder. YOUNG EVA talks to the audience.)*

YOUNG EVA
My mother and I have to sit at this kitchen table all day and whisper...we can't even move around—

MUTTI
Shhhh! *(Whispering, tense.)* The neighbors might hear you. No one can know that we're here.

YOUNG EVA *(whispering loudly)*
But I AM here—YOU'RE here! Mutti—sometimes I lie in bed at night and kick my sheets because I am so frustrated!

MUTTI
(touching YOUNG EVA's face, trying to calm her)
Oh, Evi...

YOUNG EVA
I'm 14 years old, Mutti. I want *a normal life!

MUTTI *(overlapping)*
*Shhhh! It's almost three o'clock. Mrs. Klompe will be home soon and then we can move around. Then we can talk.

YOUNG EVA
Move around? Talk??? I want to go ice skating on the canals, drink hot cocoa... I want to go back to school. I want to see my friends. I want us to be a family again. *(Beat.)* I miss Pappy. I miss Heinz.

(MUTTI brushes hair out of YOUNG EVA's eyes and embraces her.)

SOUND: Clock out

EVA

If you spent two years with one person day and night, of course you have a very, very close relationship.

So I was really my mother's everything and she was everything to me.

EVA ON VIDEO

ED

I had been to see friends who lived relatively far away, I was late coming home—

ED ON VIDEO

SOUND: Marching, truck engines

YOUNG ED

It's ten minutes past eight, ten minutes past curfew—I turn a corner within a block of my grandparents' home—and there they are: German soldiers. They don't even ask for identification—they don't have to...I'm wearing the yellow star.

ED

They didn't say much, they just...one of them took me by my arm and told me to get on the truck.

ED ON VIDEO

SOUND: Moving truck hum

YOUNG ED

I'm on this truck for about a half-hour. There's a young German guard who's holding a rifle and staring straight ahead. I know that if I'm going to escape—this is it. So I push him off balance and I jump off the truck and into the road. For one second I think I'm safe and then I look up and I see headlights coming toward me. I roll away just in time to get away from the wheels from the next truck. I get up and start running. *(SOUND: Amplified breathing.)* Running and running. I don't look back. I hide in a doorway of an apartment building where I know people. But I don't ring their bell. I just stay here for an hour or so. *(In the dark, he whistles softly from Beethoven's Ninth Symphony.)* Finally, when it's really dark, I go home.

SOUND: Truck passing

SOUND: Amplified sound of Ed breathing hard, running away

(YOUNG ED steps out of the doorway, walks cautiously down the dark, empty street. Then he stops, rips the yellow star from his coat. Then he rips a yellow star from another piece of clothing.)

ED

So the removal of the star was perhaps part of that feeling that "This is enough." In other words, "You have to risk this to get out of this in some way."

ED ON VIDEO

(The HITLER YOUTH from the first moment in the play steps forward.)

HITLER YOUTH

When I am promoted in my unit to the Hitler Youth, our leaders give me a little puppy and they tell me to keep the puppy with me day and night, to feed it and care for it, to let it sleep with me—to make it my property and responsibility. *(German Nationalist music, great fanfare.)* As the Führer has said: "We will be one people, one nation." And the youth—we are going to be *that* people and *that* nation. *Heil Hitler!*

SOUND: Nazi music

SOUND: Nazi rally

SOUND: Mass "Heil Hitler!"
VIDEO TITLE: "1944"
CHASER TITLE: "Amsterdam"

YOUNG EVA

We've been in hiding now for almost two years. Two years of having to be quiet. Two years of peeking out windows. Two years of being afraid. But today none of that matters. Today I don't feel afraid. Today is my birthday.

MUTTI *(handing YOUNG EVA a small present)*
Happy Birthday, Evi.

EVA

Eleventh May, 1944, it was my 15th birthday and I was

EVA ON VIDEO

—bit excited. My mother
and me went down to breakfast—and we were just going
to start eating when we heard
loud knocking on the door.

(YOUNG EVA and MUTTI
freeze, listen to the sound of
the knocking, the door open-
ing, boots coming up the
stairs.)

SOUND ON VIDEO: Loud
knocking, door opening,
boots coming up stairs
VIDEO IMAGE: SS Soldier
—Uniform

SS SOLDIER *(V.O.)*
Verflucthe Juden!

V.O. ON VIDEO: SS SOLDIER

MUTTI *(panicking)*
But we're just visiting, we're not Jewish!

YOUNG EVA
We haven't done anything…

SS SOLDIER *(V.O.)*
Ihr sau Juden!

V.O. ON VIDEO: SS SOLDIER

EVA
They just marched us down
the street and took us to the
Gestapo headquarters where
we were going to be interrogated. And there was no way
we could…we were just stunned into…well, we knew that
was going to be the end for
us. You know, we just…

EVA ON VIDEO

That was something we had
feared for all—all those two
years and it had happened
now.

MUTTI

We were put into a small room where other people were
waiting.

YOUNG EVA

I didn't know what to expect. I was very, very scared.

MUTTI

We waited and waited.

YOUNG EVA

And then they came for me.

(The unseen SS rip MUTTI away from YOUNG EVA.)

MUTTI

Evi!

*(A YOUNG EVA sits alone in a chair for interrogation by
two SS Nazis.)*

ACTOR ONE

What did they look like?

ACTOR TWO

What did they say?

EVA
I only remember their uniforms, and their way of speak-
ing—they were always shouting.

EVA ON VIDEO

SS NAZI *(V.O. on video)*
*Erzähle mal was du weist
und du wirst deine Mutter
bald wiedersehen.*

**VIDEO IMAGE: Cut to SS
uniform only—no faces.
This image of faceless SS
uniform will alternate
with Eva on video during
following interrogation**

EVA
"Tell us everything we want
to know and then you will
see your mother again."

EVA ON VIDEO

SS NAZI *(V.O.)*
*Du wirst deinen Vater und
Bruder auch sofort wieder-
sehen.*

**VIDEO IMAGE: SS uniform
V.O. ON VIDEO: SS NAZI**

YOUNG EVA
My father and brother?
Pappy! Heinz!

EVA
That was when I realized
that they'd also captured my
father and brother.

EVA ON VIDEO

SS NAZI *(V.O.)*
*Das ist ja klar—wir haben
deine ganze Familie hier.*

**VIDEO IMAGE: SS boots
V.O. ON VIDEO: SS NAZI**

EVA
"Of course! We have them
as well."

EVA ON VIDEO

VIDEO IMAGE: SS uniform
V.O. ON VIDEO: SS NAZI

SS NAZI *(V.O.)*
*Wie hat deine Mutter das
Geld bekommen?*

EVA
"Where did your mother
get the money from?"

EVA ON VIDEO

YOUNG EVA
I don't know! Why won't
you believe me?

EVA
The pure arrogance of them,
that they could get everything out of us that *they*
wanted, *they* were the boss.

EVA ON VIDEO

SS NAZI *(V.O.)*
Wer hat dir geholfen?

VIDEO IMAGE: SS uniform
V.O. ON VIDEO: SS NAZI

EVA
"Who helped you find
places to hide?"

EVA ON VIDEO

YOUNG EVA
I told you—I don't know! I
don't know! I don't know!

SS NAZI *(V.O.)*
*Wir werden deinen Bruder
foltern, wenn du nicht mit
uns mitarbeitest.*

VIDEO IMAGE: SS hat
V.O. ON VIDEO: SS NAZI

EVA
"We intend to torture your
brother to death unless you
cooperate with us."

EVA ON VIDEO

YOUNG EVA
No! Heinz!

SS NAZI *(V.O.)*
*Wir werden dir sogleich
zeigen was wir mit ihm
machen werden.*

VIDEO IMAGE: SS uniform
V.O. ON VIDEO: SS NAZI

EVA
"We will show you what
we will do to him."

EVA ON VIDEO
SOUND: Sustained note

*(In silence, YOUNG EVA stands, takes off her sweater,
drapes it over the chair and walks away. Talking to the
audience, looking back at the chair, it's as if YOUNG EVA
has left her body and watches while the SS Guards beat
her in the chair.)*

YOUNG EVA
They are beating me and threatening me. Eventually they
will realize I know nothing…if I knew anything I would
probably tell them. There's nothing to tell. My name is Eva
Geiringer.

Today is my birthday. I am 15 years old. This morning I woke up. I went down to breakfast to open my presents. And then they came for me.

(Knocking on a door.
Louder. Then it fades away
like a memory.)

SOUND: Knocking, louder,
fades out

EVA

The fifty years fall back
and it all comes really back
to me. It—this was really the
most horrendous experience
I've been going through. I
knew that we were all four
caught now. And we knew
about the concentration
camps. So I really had to come
to terms now with perhaps
my life was going to end there.

EVA ON VIDEO

YOUNG ED

After that night when I jumped from the Nazi truck, my grandparents just couldn't take it anymore. And even though it was very dangerous to try to escape—it was something I had to risk.

I am 16 years old. My parents have escaped from Germany and are living in Belgium. I have to try and find them. I have to try to get across the border into Belgium. But Jews are not allowed to travel, to cross borders. If I get caught, the Nazis will kill me. But if I stay... Many friends have simply disappeared. Anne and her family—are gone. Maybe they got away. Maybe I can get away too.

We arrange with a friend of the family to take me across the border. We have secret information about when it might be safe to try and cross, about when the border guards won't see us. We hide in fields. We sneak into Belgium.

Several days after saying goodbye to my grandparents, I am in Brussels. I have never been here before. My parents don't know I'm coming but I have their address. I get off the street-car, and there— *(ED'S FATHER appears.)* —on the other side of the street—there is my father. We haven't seen each other for four years.

(YOUNG ED whistles from Beethoven's Ninth Symphony to his father. At first his father doesn't hear. YOUNG ED whistles louder. His father suddenly stops, listens to the whistling. He turns and looks in YOUNG ED's direction.)

ED'S FATHER

Helmuth?

(It's as if he can't believe what he's hearing. YOUNG ED and his father walk toward each other and then run, embrace, a warm, emotional reunion.)

YOUNG ED

Father!

ED'S FATHER

How did you find us? How did you get here?

YOUNG ED

By train, on foot, on bicycle—

ED'S FATHER

But how did you get across the border?

YOUNG ED

We snuck across.

ED'S FATHER

Four years, Helmuth. We haven't seen you for four years…
Your mother won't believe how much you've grown.

YOUNG ED

Is Mother—

ED'S FATHER

She's fine. Your mother's fine. She'll be so happy to see
you.

*(He embraces YOUNG ED again and looks at his face in
disbelief.)*

ED

He was stunned at first, and
happy to see me of course.
And the underlying…the underlying feeling was always
in some way related to the
situation. Like—wonderful,
I'm happy you're here—but
what are we going to do now?

ED ON VIDEO

YOUNG EVA

After we were arrested on
my birthday, my family is
transported to Westerbork—
a transit camp…a kind of
holding camp where there
are thousands of other Jewish and Gypsy families.
Waiting. A few days later
they put us on another train.

SOUND ON VIDEO: Train

(The sound of a train starting to move very slowly. Eva's family joins YOUNG EVA on the train.)

SOUND: (NOTE: Additional sound on sound CD to play simultaneously) train

YOUNG EVA
Two days, three days…

HEINZ

Four days…

PAPPY
We don't know when it is day—

MUTTI
We don't know when it is night.

YOUNG EVA
The train is like cattle cars—

EVA
They WERE cattle cars. It was just big wagons with two iron doors. There was nothing in it whatsoever, no bedding, no nothing. We got buckets for toilet facilities.

EVA ON VIDEO

YOUNG EVA
A hundred people are pushed together in one car.

SOUND ON VIDEO: Train

HEINZ
It's so tight that we have to take turns standing—

PAPPY

Lying—

MUTTI

Sitting…

YOUNG EVA

Sometimes the train stops—

HEINZ

The doors open—

PAPPY

Bread is thrown in—

MUTTI

Buckets of water for us to drink.

HEINZ

Three days—

YOUNG EVA

Four days…

HEINZ

It's hot.

YOUNG EVA

Boiling hot.

PAPPY

And the doors are closed.

MUTTI

And bolted shut from the outside.

YOUNG EVA
Where are they taking us?

EVA *(V.O.)*
We knew we were going east but we had no idea yet where we were going to go. Nobody said anything to us.

(The train stops and we hear the same sounds from early in the play: Boots marching. Boots trampling. Dogs barking. Men shouting commands in German.)

AUSCHWITZ SS *(V.O.)*
Sau Juden! Verfluchte Mistbienen! Schnell! Schnell! Raus ihr Mistbienen. Verfluchte sau Juden!

YOUNG EVA
The train stops.

EVA
Yes. The doors of the train…

YOUNG EVA
Open…

(Sunlight floods the stage, blinding YOUNG EVA and the others.)

VIDEO IMAGE: Train tracks.
Camera pans to reveal that tracks lead to Auschwitz train stop

V.O. ON VIDEO: EVA
NOTE: Additional sound on sound CD to play simultaneously

SOUND ON VIDEO: Boots, dogs barking, German commands

V.O. ON VIDEO:
AUSCHWITZ SS

EVA ON VIDEO

VIDEO GOES WHITE

AUSCHWITZ SS *(V.O.)*
  Raus! Raus!

V.O. ON VIDEO:
AUSCHWITZ SS

YOUNG EVA
  At least we can stretch and
breathe a bit of air.

EVA
  But then we saw on the platform the big sign "Ausch-
witz" and we knew this was
the death camps. So again,
we thought, well, that's,
that's, that's it. Our last hour
was—had arrived.

EVA ON VIDEO

*(In the chaos surrounding them, MUTTI hands EVA a hat
and a coat.)*

MUTTI
Put it on, Evi.

YOUNG EVA
It's hot.

MUTTI
Wear the hat and coat, maybe they'll let you keep it.

*(YOUND EVA reluctantly puts on the hat and coat. HEINZ
smiles weakly.)*
PAPPY
You look a smart young lady now.

AUSCHWITZ SS *(V.O.)*
Männer auf eine seite.
Frauen auf die andere seite.

V.O. ON VIDEO:
AUSCHWITZ SS

EVA
"Men and women to differ-
ent sides."

EVA ON VIDEO

(PAPPY grabs YOUNG EVA.)

PAPPY
God will protect you,
Evertje.

AUSCHWITZ SS *(V.O.)*
(sharper) Männer auf eine
seite! Frauen auf die andere
seite!

V.O. ON VIDEO:
AUSCHWITZ SS

*(YOUNG EVA and HEINZ suddenly embrace. They hold
on to each other. PAPPY and MUTTI embrace one last
time. None of this is sentimental—but desperate, violent,
fast. The action OVERLAPS with EVA ON VIDEO.)*

EVA
And this is when I saw my
father and brother—saw for
the last time. And we kissed
goodbye and then we sepa-
rated. And my mother and
me went to one side and—
my father and brother to the
other side.

EVA ON VIDEO

AUSCHWITZ SS *(V.O.)*
Fünfer Reien!

V.O. ON VIDEO:
AUSCHWITZ SS

EVA
And then—

EVA ON VIDEO

AUSCHWITZ SS *(V.O.)*
Fünfer Reien!

V.O. ON VIDEO:
AUSCHWITZ SS

EVA
Another command, "Rows
of five! Rows of five!"

EVA ON VIDEO

AUSCHWITZ SS *(V.O.)*
*Fünfer Reien! Fünfer
Reien!*

V.O. ON VIDEO:
AUSCHWITZ SS

EVA
And then they…looked at
the rows of five and sorted
through—some people to
the right and some people to
the left.

EVA ON VIDEO

YOUNG EVA
The SS officer looks me up and down and finally indicates
for me to go to the left. Soon Mutti joins me.

MUTTI
Many mothers lose their daughters to the other group, to the
wrong side.

EVA

EVA ON VIDEO

All the people who went to the wrong side went straight to the gas chambers and never—were never seen again.

YOUNG EVA

I'm the youngest person left in our group. As ridiculous as I look, this hat and coat makes me look older and saves my life.

EVA

EVA ON VIDEO

We marched on into the entrance of the camp.

VIDEO IMAGE: **Sign at camp entrance**

EVA *(V.O.)*

V.O. ON VIDEO: EVA

This is the very famous picture with *"Arbeit Macht Frei"*—

YOUNG EVA/MUTTI
"Work Will Make You Free"

EVA *(V.O.)*
You know, entering Auschwitz.

V.O. ON VIDEO: EVA

EVA

EVA ON VIDEO

We were told to undress completely naked. And uh, SS was walking around freely, poking at us and looking at us and laughing.

SOUND: **Nazi commands**

YOUNG EVA *(whispering to MUTTI)*
Why are they doing this? Mutti—tell them to stop!

EVA

EVA ON VIDEO

So this was really all terrible
degradation because suddenly
we were not human beings
with a name…we were just
naked…women without name,
without belongings…

YOUNG EVA
I don't want a tattoo!

MUTTI
Shhh, Evi. *(To unseen Kappo.)* She's so young, don't do it
so strong, don't make the numbers so big.

YOUNG EVA *(tattoo number)*
"A/5272."

MUTTI
Don't hurt her, she's only a child. My child.

YOUNG EVA
Why do they have to cut all our hair?

EVA

EVA ON VIDEO
*MUTTI speaks
simultaneously*

And as well with my hair,
my mother said, *"Leave
her a little bit of hair."* And
just in the front I had a little
inch of hair which made me
look a little bit less awful.

(YOUNG EVA turns and looks at her older self and asks:)

YOUNG EVA
What happens now? What happens to me?

EVA   **EVA ON VIDEO**
You have to get up every
morning at four o'clock and
stand for two hours *appel*
which is a roll call.

YOUNG EVA
Two hours? Why will it
take them two hours?

EVA   **EVA ON VIDEO**
Because the whole camp
had to be counted and then
reported back to the SS.

YOUNG EVA
How many women are here?
A thousand?

EVA   **EVA ON VIDEO**
A thousand?!? There were
tens of thousands, perhaps
even hundreds thousands of
people.

YOUNG EVA
And I have to stand here? Why?

EVA
You will have to stand there every morning and every evening for two hours in any weather.

EVA ON VIDEO

YOUNG EVA
No talking? *(shifting nervously.)* No moving around?

EVA
No talking, no moving. If somebody sees you move you will be beaten.

EVA ON VIDEO

(YOUNG EVA stops moving, looks at her older self. She doesn't move. EVA watches her.)

VIDEO IMAGES:
1) CLOSE on photo of WOMAN IN CONCENTRATION CAMP

YOUNG EVA
It's now late in the summer of 1944 and we've been in the camp for over two months. Sleeping is almost impossible. Ten to a bed. It's itchy and very smelly. At night the bedbugs fall from the top bunks down onto anyone sleeping below. They are big, black bugs that suck your blood.

2) THREE WOMEN in same photo

3) WIDER: SEVERAL WOMEN IN BARRACKS— Same photo

4) CLOSE on ANOTHER WOMAN in same photo

MUTTI

In the morning we get some tea. That's what we get for the whole day. In the evening we get a chunk of horrible brown bread.

5) Photo of ONE CHILD behind barbed wire

YOUNG EVA

Some people try and keep part of their bread for the next day, but then people steal it in the night.

6) Photo of SEVERAL YOUNG WOMEN

MUTTI

If that happens a few times to you—you will starve to death.

7) Photo of CHILDREN

YOUNG EVA

At night we see the flames, they burn twenty-four hours. And you can smell flesh.

SOUND: Fire
8) WIDER: Photo of SEVERAL CHILDREN wearing striped uniforms, behind barbed wire

MUTTI

You can only deal with it by not believing.

LONG SHOT: Auschwitz train tracks and platform—WINTER

YOUNG EVA

We know, one hundred percent we know—but we say that such a big camp must have so much rubbish to burn, that's what's burning, and just pretend it's not true.

EVA

The shower block and gas chambers were built very similar so we never knew if we were going to go to a shower or to a gas chamber.

EVA ON VIDEO

YOUNG EVA

They tell people they are going to have a shower and they're given a bar of soap and a towel. The doors open, people are taken in, the doors close.

SOUND: Door closing

EVA

The Germans were sitting on top looking through little peepholes to see after about half a minute that people had collapsed, were lying on the floor, and were dead. And they watched that. And then after about a minute they opened the door and other prisoners, other people who were in the camp, had to take out the…the dead bodies.

EVA ON VIDEO

(YOUNG ED enters with a suitcase.)

YOUNG ED

By this time the Nazis are after the Jews in Belgium too, so my parents had made arrangements to go into hiding with a lady they know from the neighborhood who will rent a house on the outskirts of Brussels. We have no idea how long we will be there.

ED

We were there a—a total of twenty-six months.

We went into hiding in August '42 and we were liberated by the unit of the British Army on September 3rd, 1944. There's a significance in that date for me—

ED ON VIDEO

ED *(V.O.)*

—because that is the day the last transport left from Westerbork to Auschwitz with Anne Frank and her family.

V.O. ON VIDEO: ED
VIDEO IMAGE: Train
dissolve to earlier photo
of ANNE and MARGOT
FRANK
SOUND: Wind

(ANNE enters, wrapped in a blanket...she is very weak.)

ANNE

After being in hiding with Mother, Father and Margot in our Secret Annex for over two years, we were betrayed and arrested by the Nazis. We were sent to Westerbork and then put in cattle cars and sent to Auschwitz. "Men and women to different sides..." We were immediately separated from Father.

(YOUNG EVA and MUTTI enter together. MUTTI can barely stand.)

YOUNG EVA

The middle of winter. It is unbelievably cold. November, December; we have no shoes, no clothes.

ANNE

The itching. The lice. I couldn't stand it any longer. I ripped off my clothes and wrapped myself in a blanket. It's all I have.

YOUNG EVA

It's not just that we're hungry and dirty and have to work hard. It's also "Are we going to live through tomorrow?"

ANNE

December...

YOUNG EVA

January...

ANNE

Why?

YOUNG EVA

Freezing.

ANNE

My name is Anne Frank.

YOUNG EVA

My name is Eva Geiringer.

ANNE/YOUNG EVA *(together)*

I am 15 years old...

ANNE

My sister Margot and I are sent to another camp and now we're separated from Mother as well. I don't have any parents. I don't know if they're dead or alive. I think they must be dead.

*(The two young women speak, unaware of each other…
soft, lost, alone.)*

YOUNG EVA

Mutti?

ANNE

Mother?

YOUNG EVA

Pappy?

ANNE

Father?

YOUNG EVA

Heinz?

ANNE

Margot? Margot has been sick. I wish for a pencil, a scrap
of paper. A piece of bread.

YOUNG EVA

My feet are frostbit. Sometimes the blood starts to stream
through them and get a bit warm and then it hurts very, very
much.

ANNE

When I was in hiding I used to dream of sleeping under a
starry night. Now, even the moon seems cruel, hollow.

*(ANNE exits like a ghost, wrapped in her blanket. YOUNG
EVA and MUTTI huddle together.)*

ED

We didn't know exactly what was happening to the people who were being deported.

The depth of the crime and the devastation—we did not know about.

SOUND: **Wind, out**
ED ON VIDEO

YOUNG EVA

One night I wake up because something is biting on my toes. It is a rat. A big rat. It might have smelled the blood. I wish I could escape.

EVA

The chance to escape was nil. But nevertheless people did try to escape. But that was really more...out of... resignation—they'd given up. Because they were always caught. If you stepped out of line the Germans just let their dogs loose and the dogs ripped the people apart. Or they were caught and taken back to the camp. And um, then there was public hanging.

EVA ON VIDEO

YOUNG EVA

The SS people—these men—they are not much older than me. You expect people like that to look vicious—but they don't. They're boys. How is it possible for them to be so cruel?

EVA

I think it was a way of being
trained and educated. It was
a long process of several
years, to obey order, and um,
just to do what they are ordered to—to do.

There were stories going
around the camp how it was
possible that those Nazis—
the young SS boys—became
so cruel.

EVA ON VIDEO

**VIDEO IMAGE: Swastika
against red background**

(The HITLER YOUTH appears. He is nervous, uneasy.)

HITLER YOUTH

After I had the puppy for about six months, after I had kept
it with me day and night, fed it and cared for it—loved
it—we were told to report to a Unit meeting. And to bring
our puppies. Our leaders welcomed us. They praised us. They
told us we were the future of Germany. And then they ordered me to take my puppy—

NAZI *(V.O.)*
*Jetzt werdet ihy eurer
Hündchen erwügen.*

V.O.: NAZI COMMAND

HITLER YOUTH

They ordered all of us to take our puppies—they ordered us
to strangle our puppies. *(Pause.)* I…they told us if we didn't
do it—we'd never be chosen, we'd never be SS, we'd never
be real Germans. *(Pause, struggling.)* "I promise at all times
to do my duty for the Führer, so help me God." *(Beat.)* I did

it. I did what I was told. I strangled my puppy. An order—is an order. Yes? *(Mixed emotion.)* I have been a member of the Nazi youth groups since I was 7. *(Finding new strength.)* I will fight in Germany's total war. It is win—or die for Germany. *(Beat, then salutes, passionate:)* Heil Hitler!

SOUND: **Mass "Heil Hitler!"**
VIDEO TITLE: **"1945"**
CHASER TITLE:
"Auschwitz"
EVA ON VIDEO

EVA
We had of course no official news what was happening with the running of the war. But we heard airplanes, we heard shooting, and guns in the distance. And we noticed that the Germans become very nervous. And they evacuated the camp slowly, they took every day transport of people away from the camp.

SOUND: **Gunshots explosions, planes**

YOUNG EVA
One morning my mother and I wake up—

MUTTI
It is January—

YOUNG EVA
And the Germans are gone. And most of the prisoners are gone too.

MUTTI
I am too weak to go with them.

YOUNG EVA

And I won't leave my mother. There are only a handful of people like me who are able to move around. And we start to investigate the concentration camp.

MUTTI

It is very, very cold. Winter.

EVA

I was with another—a Polish woman, walking around aimlessly to look what we could find or see. We came across um, a horse which had been shot.

EVA ON VIDEO

YOUNG EVA

The horse is steaming from the heat, from the body. The first thing we think is: meat!

EVA

And the Polish woman said, "Go quickly and get a knife! We must cut into this meat right away before it gets frozen and it's too hard and we can't carve it anymore."

EVA ON VIDEO

YOUNG EVA

So I went and got a big knife and we start to cut into this horse, into the belly part. We come across something peculiar. We cut into it and suddenly we realize: it is a womb— and there is a young horse in it. I don't think I can eat that.

EVA

And she said, "Oh yes, oh yes, we'll make a very nice stew out of it." *And um… we did.* And um, when I think about this now, I think, I just can't believe it, that I really did that. But this is the way we were after eight months in the concentration camp. Food was really everything for us.

EVA ON VIDEO

YOUNG EVA speaks simultaneously

(YOUNG EVA returns to MUTTI's side.)

YOUNG EVA

Mutti, listen to me. We can't stay here like this, we don't know what's going to happen. I'm going to go to the men's camp.

EVA

We knew the men's camp was in Auschwitz somewhere near. And my mother didn't really want to let me go.

EVA ON VIDEO

MUTTI

You don't know where to go, how to find it—

YOUNG EVA

I'll find it—

MUTTI

It's too dangerous—

YOUNG EVA
I must go. I'll find Pappy and Heinz. I'll come back for you. We'll all be together again.

(YOUNG EVA kisses MUTTI goodbye.)

SOUND: Wind

EVA
Everything was covered in snow. It was very, very cold. There were no roads, no way of really knowing...but some-how I seemed to have gone in the right direction. And I walked for hours. And um. It was crossfire. I heard guns and shooting. And um. It was very, very scary. Sometimes I heard bullets flying over my head and I went to lie—low down. But eventually I arrived into the big, main camp which was Auschwitz men's camp.

EVA ON VIDEO

SOUND: Gunshot, crossfire

SOUND: Wind, out
YOUNG EVA speaks simultaneously

   And suddenly I came across a man—an old man—who stood there looking very lost. And um, he looked slightly familiar to me. And I went to him. And—he was very, very thin. Very thin head, and only very gentle brown eyes looked out of him. And we looked at each other. And he said to me,

"You look familiar. I think I
know you." I said, *"Yes!
I'm Eva Geiringer."* He said,
"I'm Otto Frank." *"Anne's
father,"* I said. "Yes, yes!
Do you know where Anne
is? Do you know where Margot is? Have you seen my
wife?" I said, *"No, no, never
saw them. Have you seen
Heinz? Have you seen my
father?"* He said, "Yes. But
they're not here anymore."

*YOUNG EVA speaks
simultaneously*
*YOUNG EVA speaks
simultaneously*

*YOUNG EVA speaks
simultaneously*

YOUNG EVA

I had found Otto Frank—Anne's father. But not my own father. Not my brother. Pappy—Heinz—they are gone. But the
possibility that they MIGHT STILL BE ALIVE, helps me
make the trip back through the snow and somehow I find my
way back to the women's camp. My mother is alive. I am
alive. Because we've had each other—we're both alive.

ED

About one o'clock in the
morning I was lying on a roof
of that—that house, and I saw
an armored vehicle turn the
corner down the road—and I
was holding my breath—and
then I saw the white star of
the allied armies.

ED ON VIDEO

SOUND: Truck engine

YOUNG ED
(calling out to vehicle) Hey!

ED

And they went another fifty
yards, turned around and came
back. And in turning around,
knocked over a telephone
pole. And stopped in front of
the house—and came in!

ED ON VIDEO

SOUND: Party crowd, music

YOUNG ED

All of a sudden there are a hundred people in our kitchen
from all over the area. A big celebration. Somebody comes in
with a bottle of cognac. A baker who has hoarded all his flour
during the war starts baking bread, we have a feast. And my
mother kisses them all!

ED

That was it. The next day
we were able to go out and
walk in the street.

ED ON VIDEO

YOUNG EVA

After Auschwitz is liberated by the Russians, it takes my
mother and I five months to return home to Amsterdam.

MUTTI

We travel by foot, by train, and by boat from Auschwitz,
Poland, to the Ukraine in Russia…

YOUNG EVA

To Odessa, across the Black Sea to Turkey—

MUTTI

Across the Mediterranean to the South of France—

YOUNG EVA

North to Paris—

MUTTI

Through Belgium—

YOUNG EVA

And into Holland.

SOUND: **Music out**

EVA

And there we stood without
any money and we had to get
to our place. So um, we just
went into a tram and asked
the conductor *could we go
free, we have no money,* we
just—well, we looked terrible anyway, we just come
from concentration camp.
And um, they didn't take
much notice but they let us
ride free. And we went back
to our apartment on the Mer-
wedeplein. There was still
somebody in it who had kept
it for us. The lady was very
happy to see us. And um...
Everything—she had left everything how it was. And it
was really weird to walk
around and see everything
how we had left it after three
years—where so much had
happened to us, we had gone
to hell and back—and there

EVA ON VIDEO

***MUTTI speaks
simultaneously***

stood all our things…un-
touched.

(YOUNG EVA stands looking at a place on the wall.)

MUTTI

Evi? What is it?

YOUNG EVA *(touching the wall)*
Pencil marks.

PAPPY *(V.O.)*
"Every month we will meas-   **V.O.: PAPPY**
ure you and see how much   **(Specific to production)**
you have grown. You'll be safe
here. We'll all be safe here."

(YOUNG EVA lingers at the pencil marks.)

HITLER YOUTH

On April 30, 1945—Adolph Hitler committed suicide. Then
Germany surrendered. *(Pause.)* The war is over. And we lost.
We've lost so much.

YOUNG EVA *(to HITLER YOUTH)*
5,860,000 Jews died in the Holocaust.

HITLER YOUTH

I was following orders.

YOUNG EVA *(pressing him)*
5,860,000 Jews died in the Holocaust.

*(The HITLER YOUTH takes off the swastika armband. He
looks lost. His words come slow, deliberate.)*

HITLER YOUTH

I promise—at all times to do my duty—for the Führer, so help—me God? *(Exits quickly.)*

YOUNG ED

My name is Helmuth Silberberg. I was born in 1926 in Germany and later moved to Holland to escape the Nazis. My nickname was Hello which was what Anne Frank called me in her diary. When I was a teenager I escaped again and hid from the Nazis in a townhouse in Belgium

ED	
My name is Ed Silverberg now. After the war I married my wife, Marlise.	**ED ON VIDEO**

ED *(V.O.)*	
We live in Hackensack, New Jersey. We have two children—	**V.O. ON VIDEO: ED** **VIDEO IMAGE: Photo of Ed and Marlise**

ED	
—and two grandchildren.	**ED ON VIDEO**

YOUNG EVA

My name is Eva Geiringer. I was born in Austria in 1929. When I was a teenager I was in hiding for 22 months in Holland. I was arrested by the Nazis and spent nine months in the Auschwitz-Birkenau concentration camp.

EVA	
After the war I married Zvi Schloss. We live in London, England.	**EVA ON VIDEO**

EVA *(V.O.)*
We have three daughters
and four grandchildren.

V.O. ON VIDEO: EVA
VIDEO IMAGE: Family photo
Eva, Zvi, Mutti and family

YOUNG ED *(to ED and EVA)*
What about Anne and her family? What happened to them?

ED
Anne's mother, Edith Frank,
died at the Auschwitz-Birkenau concentration camp.
Anne and her sister Margot
died at the Bergen-Belsen
concentration camp within
days of each other.

ED ON VIDEO

EVA *(V.O.)*
Only Otto Frank survived.
After the war, in 1953, he
married my mother.

V.O. ON VIDEO: EVA
VIDEO IMAGE: Otto and
Mutti wedding photo

EVA
We really wanted to make
a new family again.

EVA ON VIDEO

(HEINZ enters carrying a lit candle.)

YOUNG EVA
My brother—

VIDEO IMAGE: Photo of
Heinz playing the guitar

MUTTI
My son—

YOUNG EVA/MUTTI

Heinz Geiringer—

YOUNG EVA

—was evacuated from Auschwitz and forced to march to Mauthausen, an Austrian concentration camp. He died there several days before the liberation.

(PAPPY enters carrying a lit candle.)

VIDEO IMAGE: Photo of Pappy

MUTTI

My husband—

YOUNG EVA

My father, Pappy—

MUTTI/YOUNG EVA

—Eric Geiringer—

MUTTI

—was evacuated from Auschwitz and forced to march to Mauthausen. He died there several days before the liberation.

MUTTI/YOUNG EVA

They have no graves.

SOUND: Music (optional)

(ANNE enters carrying a lit candle.)

ANNE

My name is Anne Frank. I was born in Germany in 1929. I did not survive the Holocaust. I died in a concentration camp six weeks before the war was over. I was 15 years old. I did not get married. I did not have children. I did not have grandchildren. I had a diary. I dreamed of becoming a great writer.

ED *(V.O.)*

I have never forgotten the type of person she was at age 13. I imagine sometimes what she would have been like at 14, 15, or perhaps 18—and what she could have become.

V.O. ON VIDEO: ED
VIDEO IMAGE: Extreme
close-up on Anne Frank
in photo.
CAMERA SLOWLY PULLS
back on photo of Anne
Frank and continues
pull-back under Ed's V.O.

(YOUNG EVA crosses to ANNE with an unlit candle. ANNE gives her light. YOUNG EVA crosses to the same chair where she had been interrogated, drapes her sweater over the chair... She places her lit candle on the floor just downstage of the chair. She crosses upstage, taking her place in what will become a group tableau as:

HEINZ crosses to the chair, leans his guitar against it, then places his lit candle on the floor next to YOUNG EVA's. He crosses to join YOUNG EVA in the tableau.

MUTTI places the hat, which helped save EVA's life, on the chair. She lights her candle from EVA's and adds it to the row of candles on the floor. She joins her children in the tableau.

PAPPY crosses to the chair and places his eyeglasses on it. Then he adds his lit candle to the rest on the floor and joins his family who waits for him in the tableau.

YOUNG ED lights his candle from one of the burning ones and places it on the floor next to all the others. Then he removes his shoes which carried him across the border and places them with the other artifacts at the chair. He joins the group in tableau.

And finally, ANNE... She crosses to the candles, adding hers to the five on the floor. She places her diary with the other artifacts on the chair, completing the memorial. Then she crosses upstage to join the others who welcome her into the tableau.

The group looks up together from the candles to the audience.

Lights fade on the actors, leaving a pool of light on the memorial artifacts.

The lights completely fade to black, leaving only the glow of the six memorial candles to burn on through the darkness.

Silence. The play is over. The candles are not blown out.)

Alternate ending if production is done with *four* actors.

ED
Anne's mother, Edith
Frank, died at the Ausch-
witz-Birkenau concentration
camp. Anne and her sister
Margot died at the Bergen-
Belsen concentration camp
within days of each other.

ED ON VIDEO

EVA (V.O.)
Only Otto Frank survived.
After the war, in 1953, he
married my mother.

V.O. ON VIDEO: EVA
VIDEO IMAGE: Otto and
Mutti wedding photo

EVA
We really wanted to make
a new family again.

EVA ON VIDEO

(HEINZ enters carrying a lit candle.)

YOUNG EVA
My brother—Heinz Geir-
inger—was evacuated from
Auschwitz and forced to
march to Mauthausen, an
Austrian concentration
camp. He died there several
days before the liberation.

VIDEO IMAGE: Photo of
Heinz playing the guitar

(PAPPY enters carrying a lit candle.)

YOUNG EVA

My father, Pappy—Eric Geiringer—was evacuated from Auschwitz and forced to march to Mauthausen. He died there several days before the liberation.

They have no graves.

VIDEO IMAGE: Photo of Pappy

(ANNE enters carrying a lit candle.)

SOUND: Music (optional)

ANNE

My name is Anne Frank. I was born in Germany in 1929. I did not survive the Holocaust. I died in a concentration camp six weeks before the war was over. I was 15 years old. I did not get married. I did not have children. I did not have grandchildren. I had a diary. I dreamed of becoming a great writer.

(YOUNG EVA goes to HEINZ and he gives her a candle. She lights it from his. She joins the others. All four look out at the audience.)

ED *(V.O.)*

I have never forgotten the type of person she was at age 13. I imagine sometimes what she would have been like at 14, 15, or perhaps 18—and what she could have become.

V.O. ON VIDEO: ED
VIDEO IMAGE: Extreme close-up on Anne Frank in photo.
CAMERA SLOWLY PULLS back on photo of Anne Frank and continues pull-back under Ed's V.O.

(Silence. The play is over. They do not blow out their candles.)

END

LISTENING TO HISTORY

In 1996, the Indiana Repertory Theatre (IRT) produced the world premiere of *And Then They Came for Me*.

At the time, *And Then They Came for Me* was a bold experiment for me as a writer. I wanted to find a way to put history right in our laps, to not let audiences off the hook. I wanted to make the act of witnessing something more emotional, less passive; I suppose at my most ambitious, I wanted to implicate the audience as makers of history.

Another challenge was my desire to use video as part of the theatrical event—not as background, but as a major language of the play. Today, when any middle school student can make a movie using his or her smartphone, it's difficult to remember how videotape worked in 1996, when there was no such thing as "digital"—a simple change or edit took days to accomplish. Meanwhile, how were we to rehearse the timing of the play, the interaction between the actors and the video? And as the play moved back and forth between actors and the videotaped interviews of Ed and Eva, senior citizens remembering their stories from more than 50 years earlier—would audiences be able to make the required shifts in receiving story?

I'm still not sure why the play works; I'll let you make your own judgment. But *And Then They Came for Me* is my most performed play. In addition to productions all across the nation in almost every state, it has been performed around the world. It was performed in London at the House of Commons with Vanessa Redgrave hosting a command performance for political VIPs on Britain's Holocaust Remembrance Day. In one of my favorite productions, the play toured Latvia for nine months with a cast of 11 Latvian and Russian teenagers who performed the play in Latvian. None of those 11 teenagers had ever heard of Anne Frank before doing the play—that's how successful the Soviet Union had been at eliminating history, particularly Jewish history.

At the center of the play are two extraordinary human beings whom I feel privileged to know. Ed Silverberg was Anne Frank's first boyfriend; she wrote about him in her now-famous diary. During my tape-recorded interview with him in 1995, Ed would stop sometimes in mid-sentence and say, "I haven't thought about this for over 50 years." Later, I learned that he had never even told his grown children about what had happened to him during those war years.

Like Ed, Eva Schloss spent most of her adult life not talking about the war years, but eventually she began sharing her experiences with school children. In the late 1980s Eva wrote a book, and that was how her grown daughters learned the details of their mother's war experiences. In the last two decades, Eva has written two more books; she's received honorary degrees and international awards for her work as an educator and advocate for tolerance.

Now, all these years later, I can see that with *And Then They Came for Me* I was finding my way toward my own true process as a writer. Maybe it was here that I learned my deepest lesson as a writer: how to listen. Listen, listen, listen. Tell the story. And then listen some more.

—James Still

RETURNING TO THE UNIMAGINABLE

The Holocaust left an agonizing mark on the mid-20th century. This dark moment in world history resulted in the mass killing of more than six million people, vast destruction of Europe's oldest cities and the displacement of an entire generation. The event itself is a difficult one to delve into because of the unmitigated emotional cost it triggers. The atrocities are unimaginable.

This is the IRT's third iteration of *And Then They Came for Me*, having produced the play in 1996 and 2005. You, dear audience, are part of a unique local tradition, joining thousands of Indiana students and patrons who have engaged this work as witnesses. In truth, the *And Then They Came for Me* community expands beyond our home. Resonating around the globe, the play has been seen in nearly every state in the country and all over the world. The scope is large and the mission is admirable. However, in that enormous scale lays the risk of our own complacency. As we move further away in time from the actual events of the Holocaust, the danger of believing this story as a resolved or unnecessary narrative may easily tempt future generations.

And Then They Came for Me makes the "unimaginable" immediate and personal. At the heart of this story are four young adults desperately trying to make sense of their rapidly changing world. Brave, resourceful, stubborn and risk-eager, they access deep reservoirs of courage in order to survive. And like all teenagers throughout time, they want to hang out with their friends, flirt, gossip, eat junk food and rebel. The adults and rules around them heavily influence their decisions, just as they do for young people today. We root for these four, we question them, we are surprised by them and, perhaps most importantly, we empathize with them.

We return to the unimaginable because history itself isn't adequate. Making the experience of the Holocaust felt and believed is how we find the thread that connects us beyond the boundaries of time, proximity or identity.

—Courtney Sale, director
Indiana Repertory Theatre
2014 production

From Susan Kerner

Production background—

In 1994, as the director of George Street Playhouse's production of *The Diary of Anne Frank*, I witnessed the deep connection young people felt to Anne Frank's story. I was inspired to produce a new theatre piece which would place Anne's story in a broader historical context. Kristin Golden and Stephen Mosel of Young Audiences of New Jersey joined with George Street Playhouse to commission nationally known playwright James Still to begin the project. Together we envisioned a multimedia theatre piece which would connect Anne Frank's story to the lives of other hidden children of the Holocaust.

Ed Silverberg agreed to share his deeply moving memories of his family's escape from the Nazis. A boyhood friend of Anne Frank, he knocked on her door the morning the Frank family decided to go into hiding. No one answered the door, and he never saw Anne again. She was one of many friends who did not survive the war.

Eva Geiringer Schloss added her voice to the project with stories of the events which ultimately devastated her family. Eva and her mother, Fritzi Geiringer, survived two years in hiding and eight months in Auschwitz. Her father and brother died in Mauthausen days before the end of the war. Following the war, Fritzi married Otto Frank, Anne's father.

In 1995, the process of interviews, research, script development and production design began in earnest. Janet Allen lent her dramaturgical support and gave *And Then They Came for Me* its first production at the Indiana Repertory Theatre in October 1996. The George Street Playhouse/Young Audiences of New Jersey touring and mainstage productions have reached over 100,000 people since opening in November 1996.

Eva Schloss and Ed Silverberg have shared their stories with great generosity. As the Holocaust recedes in memory, it is increasingly important that their stories are heard. Eva's and Ed's presence on videotape in every performance of *And Then They Came for Me* confirms the unfathomable reality that these horrific events happened to real people in the not-so-distant past.

Bringing this project to fruition has taught me not only about history but about family, about courage and about the resilience of the human spirit. Directors give life to stories, hopefully those that make a difference in people's lives. I cannot imagine ever telling stories more important and compelling than those in *And Then They Came for Me*.

I wish to thank James Still, Diane Claussen, Kristin Golden, Barbara Forbes, Scott Killian, Stephen Datkowitz, Rob Koharchik, Gregory Hurst, Miriam Tucker, Brenda Veltre and Ann Poskocil for their passionate commitment to this work.

* * * *

Production Notes—

Pronunciation of names

The German pronunciation of Anne and Frank and the English pronunciation of Eva are preferred.

Pappy should be pronounced "Poppy."

Hello is accented on the first syllable.

NOTES